MERZ STRUCTURE NO. 2
BURNT BY
CHILDREN AT PLAY

Merz Structure No. 2
Burnt by
Children at Play

JAKE KENNEDY

BookThug 2015

FIRST EDITION

copyright © Jake Kennedy, 2015

Canada Council   Conseil des Arts
for the Arts   du Canada

ONTARIO ARTS COUNCIL
CONSEIL DES ARTS DE L'ONTARIO

an Ontario government agency
un organisme du gouvernement de l'Ontario

The production of this book was made possible through the generous assistance of the Canada Council for the Arts and the Ontario Arts Council.

LIBRARY AND ARCHIVES CANADA
CATALOGUING IN PUBLICATION

Kennedy, Jake, 1972 –, author
     Merz Structure No. 2 burnt by children at play / Jake Kennedy.

Poems.
Issued in print and electronic formats.
ISBN 978-1-77166-095-2 (PBK) – ISBN 978-1-77166-114-0 (HTML)

     I. Title. II. Title: Merz Structure No. 2 burnt by children at play.

PS8621.E634M47 2015   C811'.6   C2015-900809-3
                                                        C2015-900810-7

PRINTED IN CANADA

Table of Contents

Cezanne's Still-Life 9

A Brief History of the Cemeteries 10

A Brief History of the Tornadoes 12

The Splendid Things Are These 13

Black Ice, after Stan Brakhage 16

After Char's "The Shark and the Gull" 17

Futuromania 19

Impromptus 29

Giant Omen 57

On Discord, Please 71

Puddle with Three or Four Drops of Gasoline 72

Generic Bird on the Floor 73

Love Poems 75

The Stone Means & The Wind Means 91

Daemons, Too 92

Three Studies for Figures 94

Black to Comm 95

Elegy for Harold Ramis 100

The View from the Artist's Window 103

Magnolia Poetry Co. 104

Mishaps Or 105

After Camille Claudel's "Torso of Clotho" 108

So that lostness, eh?
That's where you have
to go in order to *survive*

—John Lent

Cezanne's Still-Life with Skull, Candlestick, & Book

Poor Yorick would speak a speech
about fucking and how to run balls-out
into the sea; how the rose once moved

this way and that in the breeze
and how the pages were always turning toward
the better future (and they were)

or something quantifiable like that
with memory's stagecraft
here stupefying all vanities—

A Brief History of the Cemeteries of
Huron County, Ontario

the rapids try to wake the barge
to at least one common fact

just as the grass
affects sea-ish poses atop the bodies

this—all of this—results
as "the final final lulling"

•

after the lapse
when resolutions have been, well, resolved

and even the darkness gives up
to a density of beige

the mason's patchwork
keeps a claim on delusion

praise
that

•

quantities of restless light
on top of the river

at once startled and then never settled
it is not like this, it is like this

for those who do or do not
reach into their past like darkened rooms

•

as for the allowances of kings
and their heinous towers—it's not theirs

only to pile up nothing and
to suffer flatness

no different than...
as special as...

...stepping stones
...wells that have been capped

A Brief History of the Tornadoes of Oxford County, Ontario

Because the future needs space
the wind makes a field

the labourer himself
and the crow further on

in order to place two keyholes
in the horizon

what gives up as the sun gives up
to obtain other reputations: down

or anyway going towards *gone*—
one does not believe in assurance

I don't at least—only vulnerabilities
as different stages of imma-blow-yer-fkin-shack-down

their threats and this relinquishing:
a cow, then a church

moving above the trees.

The Splendid Things Are These

1.
Conventionally ink
as in the abbot's enso

and not the circle pressed
on the gamer's thumb

exile and return
reconciled

and the letting of the nostalgia
(of *any* of the nostalgias) *in*

"thy flesh" as whispered
by a proponent of non-attachment

previously known as one
real mean ugly guru:

even
still

even
still

2.

Dear Dad, go fuck yourself.
Sincerely, Franz

3.

The ol' mise⁄en⁄abyme, the ol' blizzard,
the ol'...—

"at least," or this:
"given this shitty fuckin situation..."

where "" are the talons
on one of Stevens' blackbirds

above the sea
the sea as—wait for it—

that fallen theatre curtain
and the audience, rapt,

covered in its hush.

Black Ice, after Stan Brakhage

honestly what is the likelihood of mercy arriving as—say
it—your face meeting your own face on a platter of ice (great,
greater, greatest?);

when the child falls into the enclosure and the silver-backed
ape gathers her and hands her back up to her father; now,
which species is which?

layer upon layer of ice (bliss over pain over pain over bliss)
to indicate how hard it is to honour, let alone understand,
another's gift

After Char's "The Shark and the Gull"

The abandon in between objects: [knife and table] and the
much∕chittered∕about silence in | between | words as the best
idea of language; so "the shark and the gull" as two different
ways to look at the pitiless setting: "the sea and the sky"—
neither of which can speak; the original words are *mother, not,*
what, man, and the verb *to hear*

Futuromania

for NFP

As soon as someone dies, (there is a) frenzied construction of the future (shifting furniture, etc.): futuromania.

—Roland Barthes

Where is the source of light? *It varies, as the gnomen. It transports the object in the form of a shadow. It is the object; this is what we will call the miracle.*

—Robin Blaser

1.

all so's [conversational]

humbled by the suddenness of darkening:

a blown fuse—

as if a shadow-house replaced the current one

when hearing the name "Lorca" or "Wal-Mart"—

immersed in the great and inconsequential alike,

elegy *and* mashed potatoes

.

2.

for instance, [matter of fact] two bees trapped under a coffee
    cup—

a description of Vincent's left ear at Arles—

then a scene of miners whispering within the collapse—

to long for, now, what?—

an immediate redemption—

any mode of release—

or more of that/the same fear in order to escape the fear of soon
    having to escape a newer fear—

3.

of Flaubert to Colet, [epistolary]

as in "Because I always sense the future,

the antithesis of everything

is before my eyes"—

this, then, as well:

the struck match that

cues a greater darkness, too

4.

gallows in the public square—[informational]

for those who would explore "doings"

the head (offered like a lantern)

ultimate survivor (our useless desire as trunk)

in its own nakedness and passivity:

a guillotine that says "I'm not hungry anymore!"

and longs not to say

5.

that red apple is twisted [avuncular] in two by that farmer's
   hands

the split itself means appetite:

good or bad or *or?*...

only in this (the or) do I have everything to say /

and only in this am I saying it:

the split is the materialization of the *predicament:*

seek out that nothing!

6.

list alleyway microwaves, list the elegance of cigarette foil, list
    assholes pressed on photocopier glass—[categorical]

what is 'I' doing (anything *better?*) when it types…

in time?

what is 'I' doing when it types in time anything better?—

each second, wait!—

the poet's ethics:

to want to live but only in order to write a little better!

7.

as when chance trumps chance by sending the playing cards
     out of the shuffle and into the air [playful]

a wind inside the curtains that looks fake while the fan's breeze
     appears real

next it's words leaving the bedroom window

heading on into other mouths in other bedrooms

and in *their* order

with the original lovers saying:

come back / to us / soon /

8.

neither accept nor denunciate a longing for wholeness—
    [didactical]

beyond rivalries, at least—

without its own stomach—

some (as yet) great, unhungry solitude

the yippee⁄ki⁄yay of the wordless—

let that wanting be for contraries

that there are right and true directions but only   not | for | us

Impromptus

Compare

misery

to

wolves

Measure glory with "face"

Insert
    a liver in
place of
    a book

Accept

art

as

hysteria

Zoom in on Tarr's terrorized cat

X-ray
the X-ray
to get V.
Borge

Surround

any rose

w/ meat

Suffer

as paper

above

flame

After
Twombly
you are
what?

Weigh language against bullies

Whirl
fishing
line on
a rib
bone

Fasten

teeth

onto

outré

ideas

Frame

scars

Giant Omen

1. That It Is Madness to Judge the True and the False from Our Own Capacities

So there could be a party for the celebration of our absurd expectations...—*please join us for The Brittle Years and for the recitation of the elegy entitled "Our Finest Earlier Pronouncements or Boy Are We Jerks"*—with all the guests holding crystal Y's: their empty questions, really—which (let us) fill with sand or the guts of watches or Kool-Aid—ah, the best writing says: we are stupid *and* beautiful, keep it up!

2. On Educating Children

If only the teacher had reached into *Mad Max 2 (The Road Warrior)* and plucked the hourglass from Pappagallo—and smashed an "it"—at dawn, say—on the pavement so that living meant the freeing of time rather than the loss of—to show *that* to the seeds.

3. On Habit: And On Never Easily Changing a Traditional Law

Always in costume? Perhaps (what?) when Neil has the archer split the tree, in that ver|y|sim|plic|i|ty, there is the obliteration of all laws... the uncovering of the habit of habit. But not an originary exposure—no pure birthing grounds. Just: *here* is one other way to get through.

4. One Is Punished for Stubbornly Defending a Fort Without Good Reason

In K.'s hands, though, there would be (this) fundamental misunderstanding: the lone defender of the tower wishes (in truth) to forfeit the keep... but all of his (it must be) gestures of resignation/surrender are read as hostilities. Therefore, K. is the hero of our melancholy. And his predicament is the only authenticity.

5. On Fear

The body (it might be Lorca's?) gives up to (as if entirely *for*)
the photograph: throwing the arms out like this; I suppose (in
order to release) fear confesses, too; by this I mean the blasé lake
terrifies the car—calls to it with its matter-of-factness.

6. That the Taste of Good and Evil Things Depends in Large Part on the Opinion We Have of Them

We of the backgrounds or the middle-scapes, we finally earn the right to move towards a word like mercy or it arrives to us—though not... floating down like a cherry blossom but rather tied to the stick-leg of a pigeon and the message reads: *the torment's only in the approach*—

7. On Prognostications

Just once—he said—let the shape of all the crows become a page covered in corrections upon corrections until the only clarity is that gathering, intelligent darkness.

8. On Liars

What hurts, what feels truest is (tell us!) that one's suffering is the unabashed purpose of joy. The best thing is to watch the will of the wind distribute your papers out over the water—but not name it. Do not name it!

9. On Idleness

Whatever. Is it grotesque? This here lugubrious spirit-bile: coffee in a glass mug. Milton's or Montaigne's or Baudelaire's or Dickinson's or YOUR PLUMBER's gloomy lassitude—on the inevitable park bench? in any ill-lit bedroom? At the same time, say, even at the top of a bona fide mountain, well... what else should we be doing at such moments?

10. We Reach the Same End by Discrepant Means

Better still if there could be a sparrow in place of the old thumping It. One might just open a small door in the ribs, let the heart fly around the room for a while.

On Discord, Please

this would seem to be important:
the competing directions also want

desire to manifest tension:
leaving two holes at the temples

where tissue means
threshold and restriction

these O's at the side of the head
are homage to what cannot be completed

Puddle with Three or Four Drops of Gasoline

Trying to get to the future tense
and hold on to the *here*
resulted in renunciation:

spilled kaleidoscope, residue of
time travel at light-speed—
hokey-ass sci-fi elongations of beings

Okay—renegade rainbow
moral-less joy-explosion
the pavement's fucked sunrise:

what Hamm sees:
zero + zero + zero.

Generic Bird on the Floor

The singe is the finest vestige
and what the fuse sacrifices for *bam*
the chameleon knows too
always erasing itself just as it arrives

•

how the window becomes
shark's teeth in all these afterwards
oh, to enter that room and
describe a single absence fully—

•

wind or sky or air or glass:
to be in any way worthy
of this offering: that which shows
all the gone

Love Poems

Composition 2

To be all, especially a body. Look, as a well has coherence but no singleness of focus; nothing within it (you) is irrelevant. The body as array; you have a wish to make a thread fused to another: ordering them, you give the way you want, while the other, ordinary body deals with its singleness by focusing attention on time. In other words, you lose the "logically"— you look to unity to be irrelevant digressions and unnecessary shifts in points of view: "you" as rearranging body: your disrupted singleness: a wish in a well.

Composition 3

Placing one sentence after another only guarantees that "you could still come apart." In fact, one can only be writing you in two ways: 1. the transitional you; and 2. the you that contributes to the development of another you. Coherence is transitional material and writing is always writing apart. You achieve you because of because, if, or, and, could, and after... You are a linking, you are an all ways, you are the ideas of ideas, you are simply a one and a two and a you and an another you. You are only.

Composition 4

a) Beginning

A hook never closes; at least in relation to the body, it will be
open even beyond the end. A hook, then, is the promise that
every death is a beginning or every beginning is a death just
beginning or... Good. It will be the task of all nature to not
tamper or diminish the function of this mystery.

b) Middle

It is as if you are words—a kind of writing above images, or
that is only images. How you are death and then not death
because you yourself explain the poem's material questions:
what statement is best to show moving through space, through
time, and from physical composition to composing thought?
The words are you, you, and you. The words are your selves or
a will shaped as your body. So what would you have death or
a poem do? Reach for that kind of idea? For a you above all the
print and data?

c) Ending

The development of your new light, here, is not for its own
sake. In other words, your light is usually abandoned to
someone else. It repeats something as you will do so in order to
help all others be whole. Inevitably, growing out of the light
is the ending of the light. Consciously, naturally, you do that:
introduce a beginning to conclude a conclusion. Your light
knows just where it is going.

Composition 7

b)

The main weakness of writers is to settle for coherence when
words long for (are a form of) splintering. You find yourself,
your you, in small parts—as you should.

c)

Each piece of you contains many characters: lions, monarchs,
eggs. I write to tell the machine that mystery. For example, I
will write: I am attending university so that I can learn more
about myself and the world—and especially about you. So far
I have learned that I, like the looking glass, am not doing the
words but am being done by them. Recently, I also learned that
there is in each 1, 2, 3, 4 a strong reversal in thought and body:
4, 3, 2, 1. Like Hamlet, I know that the earth always muddies
the heaven of the body. But I want to tell a friend about your
beauty as if an anchor was the sun. A person can be told: try to
lose to try to be true. But that sounds stupid in real life. In order
to dream you, I have to assume that beauty is the body moving
in both mud and sunlight.

What does time lose as it illustrates its permanent rules?—only
that a week, a day, an hour have failed because they cannot keep
you.

T.

If it can't remember: it's sky.
If memory needs a thing there's
the lake and what it holds below.

The tunnel stands for permission
that the train might
just bring its passengers into a clarity.

In the next dream the clouds are duhs
and the stones opt for ascension:
aspen‑tall.

And it would be great to have remoteness
freed from every instance
of time—i.e., standing over here

might mean there, what's ahead,
and you, too.

In and Out of the Shadows

The spring worms are here.
There are no laws for books,
no laws for worms, either.

The lamp that puts light right there
and not over there or there
is hallowed because indifferent.

As when the viewer is before a painting
and the painting exists
for that shared singularity.

As when the fridge
same-olds a door of light
onto your bluish wall and one might just get through—

What's There Is There, Again

Holes are words
that came true
leaving (*needing to leave*) nothing

As "this" remains
only in the idea
of water coring through the book

The splendid discourse of
"was," too, this Hepworth O,
with really no pity for what it cut away

I think when you think
it makes actions
in the parts of the landscape I like best

You as a what has happened
and you as a had to
and a will always

Late Letter from Croisset
for BB

honest words exist
in some "right now"

& who couldn't use
big landscapes to confess to

such as a field
with cauliflowers in it

just to say "hey, brains,
every newness is a mourning"

if only to forget
the literary baubles

kick against
our advanced training

and honour the sea
by despising poetry

as in a puddle
that keeps ringing

an alarm for the turning
of certainties into uncertainties

to say what's lost
right at the moment one receives any "more"

Hurtin' Poem with Abstract Bee

It says "prepare for me"
by sizzling the air—
as if the telephone wire's a lit fuse.

Its narrative is a kind of despair
carried in susurrations
which are *muttering our blues*

a.k.a. the orders of retreat:
zzz's that force verbs to convert
all action into—yep—torpor, pain.

Anyway, so what? It's just
a whisper. It means *hurt*
then *more of it*—then *more, again.*

No More Love Poems or If Only This Poem Played at the Knitting Factory Circa 1998

"The narrative directionality of myth"
is the just the kind of sentence
that a chestnut tree blooms against

and tells the audience
in a pop song that such flowering branches
are merely white flower things and not a tree of bells

even Eurydice is dullsville in truth
until you arrive inside the wind
with none of the theatre⁄y gusts

just being a "scent in the air"
which shakes the chimes
which also shakes the tree

and the flowers ring for what's unaffected
for how boring love is
for how banal in its totality

how blessedly indifferent
to your allness,
for just what is.

Rain

Not having to prove anything
it means loss⁄as⁄loss⁄that's⁄all

as in "while we are *for* the sufferers,
we will not lend ourselves *entirely* to their conditions"

lucid enough pocks, at least
to see one's worst seconds falling

to which life responds: mobilizing worms
who connote calm but are actually losing their shit

"such grim equilibriums"
as if rain talks like that

falling for one's general disasters, big
successes or inevitable public declawings

this weather appears: the theatre
of the clattering ellipses

The Stone Means & The Wind Means
for JD

The stone means "what does not belong"; detachments, sure:
each stone is the measure—that much more certain of itself
than any old knuckle of rock; these sentences, such as "there is
nothing so self-aware as…" lead language towards the object
as if it were waiting for hard harder hardest grammar; and
it's a consequence, too: of flawed patience; there, modest as a
lozenge—unutterable freedom; less and more sadness (both) if
Drummond de Andrade is filmed tapping a pebble from his
loafer; or someone sucks a rock in order to outwait hunger; I
suppose it's a desert, too, vast in its resolute localness

•

As in the wind kicking open the front door, its impulse is only
to provide vastness a taste of constriction: "hey, check out this
cell…" the fury is the storm's pleasure at testing wall as "wall,"
ceiling as "ceiling"; or the house is merely a cube and the giant
doesn't understand cubes and therefore all beauty could be lost
unless poetry is used to really *communicate*; the most sublime
thing would be to get a tattoo of a chrysanthemum and after
the inferno, pluck this flower from one's forearm and just hold
it up for a while in the air

Daemons, Too

Kmac, it's devilish:
knowledge degrades

and degrades and
the unknowables one wants

well, they remain
unknowable

the only priority is
getting to it, some thus

as in a gull standing *thusly*
on a bronze head

and then perched *thusly*
on some bronzed book

the laws read
waiting sucks

and the laws are called
shit for brains

made specifically
to refuse to signify at all

so the monument (who knows!?)
is its own latrine

or something which means
the difficulty of getting history to care about us

see the divine white⁄splatter?
This is the reproof.

Three Studies for Figures at the Base of the Crucifixion,
(after Francis Bacon)

We (Ass⁄Mouth, Hand⁄Maw, lo the Pig⁄Shudderer)
Repurposed shithouse lumber for the corpse⁄cart
They call our trundling the reverse art
& don't we speech the speech of mutterers

backward lyric⁄ing murderers
praise the rats, the worms, & the sheeny rooks
that tore the bodies and shook
the meat free of its wooden girders

all for the happier & happiest surfeit:
soon dusk, soon night, soon eclipse—all to exit.

Black to Comm

1.

When it's morning there are hyphenated words: blah⁄stars,
rookie⁄sun; let their stitches reunify the run⁄over dog; the
road itself gives then cancels too much hope; when it rains
in French poems such chains are repurposed links meant to
attach themselves to the shoulders of busted folks and lift them
back up in the requisite dream scene; or frantic at the perimeter
of puddles—in grief over the cut worm—I swear the robin
labours to coax it back together; against the cynical "as ifs," as
if all recompense was possible

2.

When it's whole the fingers lock together and the sign for kerpow is this: move the right hand east and the left hand west until the prayer is in fragments; so much cannot be seen / that. at. least. is. ob.vious... in its way *too* clear; jazz⁄hands also mean falling snow and that each body is comprised of war⁄bling atoms: a ceaseless seizuring; the shading⁄over⁄the⁄notepad trick, applied to a "your life," reveals all the traceries of hurt; trauma's only joke (revealed letter by letter): Y O U ' R E S T I L L F U C K E D; so much can't be said, even stupid things, especially stupid things

3.

When it's most real the deviation triumphs: Čapek's robot is
too good at not being itself; the test is "can the grip solve the
stem of the champagne glass?"; it can, just as the silver-backed
ape restores the child to the parent and then returns to its own
slump; "it's all so fucking depressing" is a phrase for distances:
so and so's poems mumbled in a Vladivostok boxcar; that
which we have no right to speak of and therefore keep speak-
ing about; excuse me, when it's most unsayable it insists on its
transmission; the actors achieve the sea by billowing a length of
blue cloth; the waves mean the lovers cannot hear each other's
confessions; carry, oh buoyant words—but as a better silence

4.

When it's work Larkin does toad-at-desk until it's difficult
to tell the typewriter from the shit-kicked torso; lumped and
humped by the hours, too; tree-rings that tell the time as whorls
on the perp's fingerprints: this means you are an old farmer
/ this means you're a young buck adept at spreadsheets; the
burlap-hood around the sentenced ones or how the Burger
King crown weighs on the part-timers: both are obscene
honours; whatever, wherever—why go at it/why go to it; oh,
curse the way that Sylvester stages his mouth as a mouse hole

5.

When it's failure the clock goes *sproing* and yet the cuckoo is liberated; into what freedoms might it wander; the elegists are trying to find a way towards earnestness even though they know that you know that they know that you know that that way is not earnest enough yet…; surely, as the impossible heap, them or him or she as sack of bones, surely then it'll be okay to say "I mean it, I really mean it"?

Elegy for Harold Ramis

Oh! You're here. Oh, this is big, Peter. This is very big.
There's definitely something here. It's moving! It's here. It's
a woman. Ready. I wouldn't say the experience was com-
pletely wasted. Based on these new readings, I think we have
an excellent chance of actually catching a ghost and holding
it indefinitely. I'm always serious. Just for your information,
Ray, the interest payments alone for the first five years come
to over $75,000. It's 9,642.55 square feet. Our courteous and
efficient staff is on call 24 hours a day to serve all your super-
natural elimination needs. Print is dead. Is that a game? I
collect spores, molds, and fungus. I think it's the food of the
future. She's telling the truth—or at least she thinks she is. Or
even a race memory, stored in the collective unconscious. And
I wouldn't rule out clairvoyance or telepathic contact either.
You're a Scorpio with your moon in Leo and Aquarius rising.
Did you see anything? I blame myself. We'd better adjust our
streams. Something was definitely here. Were you recently in
the bathroom? The wet towels, residual moisture on your lower
limbs and hair, the redness in your cheeks indicating... When
you were in the bathroom, did you notice anything that was
yellow and unusually smelly? Ray! Where are you? Are you
all right? Ray! It's here! It just went into the Banquet Room on
the third floor. Wait! Wait! There's something I forgot to tell
you. Don't cross the beams. Trust me. It will be bad. It's hard
to explain, but try to imagine all life as you know it stopping
instantaneously and finding yourself confined forever in another
dimension. Don't cross them! Watch it! Easy... Easy... I'm

going to throw in my trap now. He's in here. They're not guns. They're particle-throwers. I couldn't do that. You might hurt someone. On Earth—no. But on Krypton we could slice him up like Oscar Mayer Bologna. Neutronize. System shut. I've got to sleep. I'm worried, Ray. It's getting crowded in there. And all my recent data points to something big on the bottom. Well, let's say this Twinkie represents the normal amount of psychokinetic energy in the New York area. According to this morning's PKE sample, the current level in the city would be a Twinkie 35 feet long weighing approximately six hundred pounds. Bring him inside, Officer. I am Egon, Creature of Earth, Doctor of Physics, Graduate of M.I.T. Yes, have some. Vinz, what sign are you waiting for? Hello? What is it? Does she want to be? Some. I just met the Keymaster. He's here with me now. Venkman? Are you there? I agree. All right. I'll try. All right, Peter. Good night. Die in what sense? I don't care. I see us as tiny parts of a vast organism, like two bacteria living on a rotting speck of dust floating in an infinite void. You have nice clavicles. I wonder where Stantz is. I think we're going to need him. You can see what's inside through the monitor if you wish. He wants to shut down the storage grid. No... no water. There's nothing you can do. The storage facility blew. This one... shut off the protection grid. Oh, shit! If you don't shut up I'm going to rip out your septum. And look at this, Peter. Cold-riveted girders with selenium cores. Of course! Ivo Shandor, I saw his name in Tobin's Sprit Guide. He started a secret society in 1920. Yes. After the First World War Shandor decided that society was too sick to survive. And he wasn't alone. He had close to a thousand followers when he died.

They conducted rituals, bizarre rituals, intended to bring about the end of the world. Who? You talked to Gozer? Sumerian—not Babylonian. What is it? I don't believe in luck. Thank you. It's Shandor—the architect! Not necessarily. I think he's saying that since we're about to be sacrificed anyway, we get to choose the form we want him to take. That appears to be the case. No. Full-stream with strogon pulse. No! Them! Shoot them! Cross the beams. Life is just a state of mind.

The View from the Artist's Window

A torched wheat field
children walking under the willow
two seahorses, bobbing, on the hull of a cello
a mother made of mist
one pneumatic-message capsule, empty
the wind hysterical in a laundry line
a Citroën, some vivid moss, and the slugs.

To the east, the family home of Choisy-le-Roi
the walk-inside-able book written by the scholar who
     understood all history as mirrors
the New York Public Library in blue air
porridge pushed through a slot
plus particles in the cosmic void
then shark's teeth/the broken teacup/Chauvet spearheads
and the sticky note on a refrigerator: "I give up."

Magnolia Poetry Co.

What's wanted is beyond desire,
acting for itself—as it should

"it" is meant to be an epiphany
at the end of so-and-so's ho-hum sorrow

or for those who glint noon off a knife blade
in order to hypnotize the charging bear

and communicate with starfall, because
some of us down here understand the soul

but don't want to say the word
we prefer the window with a baseball moving through it

those moments that are for objects alone
how they, the things, are embarrassed

that we need to speak at all.

Mishaps Or

1.

The snapping, relentless wind in *Kagemusha/Shadow Warrior*
when the double (a commoner/thief) of Shingen (a revered
warlord of the Takeda clan) is first revealed: astonishment as
the rippling of those cloth walls!

2.

Galeano believes in language. We do not believe in language.
We have not had to believe in language... asked, maybe, to live
the very opposite: that language does nothing at all.

3.

Reconciliation or concord / grief or the cantankerous: when the
artwork is all dovetails (grace) / when the artwork is all detritus
(shame)... the real, says Joanne, being both...

4.

The red paint—brush strokes stylized as blood—of the 1970s
Westrex logo... as a mark of Zatoichi's legacy (which is a
word that seems to include all three stages of linear time: past,
present, future)... similarly, how Zorro would mark the wall
or wound a man with his zagging initial...—O these men /
these men—... their fear of loneliness? their courage to endure
it? apparently searching for the art that can slash the letter in the
very air?

5.

"Yet much is left, although all is already written"—Mina Pam
Dick; the only real that interests K. is that which has already
been enclosed in the artwork; for instance, Goethe's etching
of the owlet perched on the severed head: it's reason vs. desire
or it's what⁄I⁄did vs. what⁄I⁄thought or it's a record of wild
dependencies: the shadow that needs the light which needs the
shadow and all that.

6.

In order to show the difference between this now⁄world and
that future⁄world the sci⁄fi film requires the scene in which
gravitylessness allows the future⁄worlders to bounce⁄glide
throughout their day—everything else is the same except, there,
they float while shopping.

7.

Guy Maddin's *Paradise Lost, Book 1*

8.

& deep pity for the emaciated cow, my spirit animal: pinned, at
its ass, to the past...

9.

If we had to point at an authentic yes: the tree that concedes to
fall in order to span the river.

10.

Bill Morrison's *Decasia* film: on the left-hand side of the screen a turn-of-the-century boxer who punches directly towards the right-hand side of the screen which is the undulating, decaying, warbling film: a fight with the ghost of time.

After Camille Claudel's "Torso of Clotho"

Has he changed your sand today? "what falls," reads the tree's
decree, "is what's resisted too long, anyway"—this interests
her: so many varieties of release; in the television advertisement
for espresso the woman closes her eyes to signify both fuck you
& bliss; thus the defiance: to be neither for nor against time
but within it; her torquedness: the pleasure of craning to. see.
what's. coming

•

Too much rain / not enough rain / and these robins are actually
tugging out the most reluctant of earth's better ideas; exits /
emergences—*it's all the same fkin day, man*; aha, her torquedness;
she seems to be looking directly into the sun as if it were a drain
for light: yes, we too are for extinguishing

Acknowledgements

"Futuromania" appeared in *Capilano Review* and won the Robin Blaser Award. Some of the "Giant Omen" pieces appeared in *LIT* (USA). "Cezanne's Still-Life with Skull, Candlestick, & Book" appeared in *The Awl* (USA).

Jake would like to thank the BC Arts Council, Okanagan College, and The Banff Centre for the Arts for all of their respective assistance. He would also like to thank the Tirten Tirten Collective. Lastly, Jake would like to thank, and heartily, the mighty beautiful living giving thing that's BookThug.

Jake Kennedy is the author of two poetry collections: *The Lateral* (2010) and *Apollinaire's Speech to the War Medic* (BookThug, 2011). His work has appeared in literary journals across Canada, the US, and the UK, including *The Capilano Review, McSweeney's Internet Tendency*, and *The Awl*. Kennedy is the recipient of the bpNichol Chapbook Award for *Hazard* (BookThug, 2007), the Robert Kroetsch Award for Innovative Poetry for *The Lateral*, and the Robin Blaser Award for Poetry for the long poem "Futuromania" (2011). He also received a BC Arts Council Writing Grant in 2013. Kennedy lives in Kelowna, BC, where he teaches English literature and creative writing at Okanagan College.

Colophon

Manufactured as the first edition of *Merz Structure No. 2 Burnt by Children at Play* in the Spring of 2015 by BookThug

Distributed in Canada by the Literary Press Group www.lpg.ca
Distributed in the US by Small Press Distribution www.spdbooks.org

Shop online at www.bookthug.ca

BOOK
PRODUCTION
WAR ECONOMY
STANDARD

Type + design by Jay MillAr
Copy edited by Ruth Zuchter
Cover image by Jake Kennedy and kevin mcpherson eckhoff